Financial Management

A guide for non-financial managers and directors in the NHS

Financial Management

A guide for non-financial managers and directors in the NHS

Roy C. Lilley
Chairman
Homewood NHS Trust

Foreword by Rennie Fritchie

RADCLIFFE MEDICAL PRESS
Oxford and New York

©1994 Radcliffe Medical Press Ltd.
15 Kings Meadow, Ferry Hinksey Road, Oxford OX2 0DP, UK

141 Fifth Avenue, New York, NY 10010, USA

British Library Cataloguing in Publication Data
A catalogue record for this book is available from the British Library.

ISBN 1 85775 072 1

Typeset by AMA Graphics Ltd., Preston
Printed and bound in Great Britain

Contents

Foreword

It is very rare that a 'guide' is a good read. Mainly because the author opts either for a detailed stage-by-stage approach or chooses the dip-in-to mode, which has little continuity.

This book is that rare exception. Managing to do both while remaining simple in language and balanced in content. Breadth and depth are combined on a subject which is both timely and important.

It is essential that managers and non-executive directors understand the context and the formulae which relate to finance in the NHS as a prerequisite for *not* getting bogged down in the detail.

Since the inception of the NHS reforms, managers and non-executive directors without a financial background have been asking one recurring question – 'but what does it all mean?' This book helps us to answer that question and to become all the more effective in serving the NHS.

Rennie Fritchie
Chair
South Western Regional Health Authority
March 1994

1

Introduction

NHS Trust Boards exercise the freedom to lead their organizations to success by powers granted to them under the NHS and Community Care Act 1990.

Different Trusts will have different yardsticks for success, but overall, 'success' for the NHS means something which encompasses quality; outcomes for patients, residents and clients; happy and secure work opportunities for staff; and value for money for the taxpayer. This is no easy task!

Trusts must achieve all this within the framework of public accountability; Boards must deal with issues of financial management, audit and integrity and be answerable for their actions.

The proper financial management of a Trust is at the heart of achieving success. No matter how creative the planning and no matter how hard the team of directors, managers and staff are prepared to work, unless the financial facts add up, success will not be on the agenda. Indeed, embarrassing failure may be staring the Board in the face.

For the directors of the newly created NHS Trust Boards, many will find financial matters difficult to grasp. Not only non-executive directors, but also executive directors, whose specialty is not finance, may find 'finance' difficult to master.

However, the Board as a whole is responsible for the financial performance of the Trust – not the financial director alone. It is vitally important that every member of the Board has a sound grasp of what is required of them. This guide seeks to demystify finance, for the non-financial director and manager.

2

Organizing the
Trust Board

There are three fundamental questions to ask when organizing the Trust Board.

- Does the Board properly understand what its role is?

- How will meetings be scheduled and business conducted?

- Will the Board be able to demonstrate that it has taken its decisions properly?

The role of the Board

Separating out the duties of the executive function of the Board from the non-executive function seems to cause a great deal of confusion. The answer to the 'who does what' question is simple.

Being a director of a Trust is a role of 'status' and not 'function'. It is the difference between managing the organization and pointing it in the right direction.

Having the status of non-executive director confers no functional role in the organization; the non-executive director has no managerial responsibility.

The picture for the executive director can be more confusing. A nurse director or medical director will have a managerial responsibility, as well as the same responsibilities as the non-executive director for the direction of the organization as a whole.

The executive and the non-executive director both have the job of pointing the organization in the right direction, but the executive director will have the additional responsibility of ensuring that the wishes of the Board are carried out.

If there is a confusion in roles, it is the executive director who has the confusion and not the non-executive director. The non-executive director will be invited to join the Board to bring an independent perspective and vision to the Trust and to keep it focused on its objectives. The executive director will be recruited to the organization for his/her skills and talents, as a manager, to deliver the plans and visions agreed upon by the Board. It is very likely he/she will have no experience of a boardroom setting.

There will be times when, because of the special experience and talents of the non-executive director, he/she may be called upon to help deliver the executive agenda of Trust. This is most likely to happen in the early days of Trust status, when the Board is managing the changes in the organization needed to move it from one run by a command structure from the centre, to a contract organization run for the benefit of its customers. The business experiences and skills of the non-executive director can be of special value and it is important that ways are found for this experience to be brought into the organization, shared with the Board and benefited from by everyone.

also be the permanent 'attendance register' to show who has been diligent in their attendances at meetings and who has not.

THE MINUTES

The minutes of the last meeting should be read and approved as a true record of the business transacted and the decisions made at the last meeting.

The minutes of the previous meeting should be circulated to all members of the Board (regardless of whether they were present), as soon after the last meeting as possible.

The chairman may take the view that it is not necessary to read through the minutes of the last meeting line by line and in detail. However, he/she should give members of the Board the opportunity to challenge the record of the meeting if it is in any way inaccurate and does not properly reflect what was said or decided.

MATTERS ARISING

The minutes of the last meeting are bound to contain issues that have been actioned or carried forward into the current meeting cycle. Matters arising is not a 'catch all' spot, but a particular opportunity to follow up on what was supposed to have been done – it may be compared with a 'things to do' list, and the chance to check off what has been done, or find out why there have been variations in what was expected but not achieved.

FINANCE

More of this in detail later. Nevertheless, in brief, the financial report should include an analysis of expenditure against budget and income from contracts and notes on any changes or deviations from the expectations set out in budgets fixed at the beginning of the financial year. Some Trusts (in common with usual practice in the private sector) are able to provide a monthly balance sheet – to measure the progress of the organization against the expectations set out in the business plan. In addition, there should be a summary of the cash that the Trust has available to it and how much it is likely to need. All of this information should be compared on a month by month basis. This will enable the Board to plot the financial progress of the Trust and to see if the income is being collected promptly, how much the Trust owes to others, if bills are being paid on time and if there is enough cash in the organization to enable it to meet its obligations.

The information should also include how the Trust is performing in its contracts. Is it keeping up-to-date with its workload; is it pacing itself properly; will it run out of work or money, or both?

Some forecast of the Trust's future position can also be expected – usually a commentary about future projects and their progress.

The whole of the reporting framework should reflect the Trust's business plan. This document drives the organization. Delivery of the business plan is vital and the reporting structure should ensure that there can be an early warning if a plan or project is being blown off course, or targets will not be met.

SPECIFIC ITEMS

Specific items on the agenda, that is to say not the routine financial items for report, will vary from Trust to Trust. Certainly some regular report from the human resource or personnel department is likely, as will be an update on the progress of specific projects.

It is important that the Board remembers it is in place to direct the organization and not to manage it.

ANY OTHER BUSINESS

This part of the agenda needs careful handling if it is not going to become a free for all. Some Trusts do not operate an 'any other business' slot and it is difficult to see, with a properly constructed agenda, why 'any other business' has a place. Some Trusts find it useful to end meetings with an 'information exchange'. The chairman will invite each member of the Board to speak for three or four minutes on a subject of information, or concern, or perhaps a meeting or conference they have attended (or perhaps just 'gossip'), that may be of interest to other members.

3

Fact File

Summary of the basics

THE SECRETARY OF STATE REQUIRES EACH TRUST TO:

1. Produce an annual business plan.

2. Publish an annual report on the Trust's performance.

3. Publish a set of annual accounts, independently audited.

The Management Executive (ME) of the Department of Health has a limited range of options open to it to interfere in a Trust's affairs. These options are called reserve powers. Reserve powers will only be used in the most exceptional circumstances. If a Trust recognizes that it is getting into trouble during the course of a year and its long-term viability is at risk, it has a duty to inform the ME.

DURING THE COURSE OF THE YEAR A TRUST MUST:

1. Provide information required by Ministers, to support the public accountability of the NHS as a whole.

2. Provide annual reports under the AIDS (Control) Act.

3. Provide financial monitoring information; monthly, quarterly and annually, as required.

4. Submit major capital schemes for 'approval in principle', for Treasury approval.

TRUSTS ARE OBLIGED TO:

1. Comply with legal and any other requirements of statutory bodies. They do not enjoy Crown Immunity.

2. Comply with European Community Directives.

3. Comply with 'hazard and safety' notices issued by the ME and other government departments.

4. Comply with advice and guidance notices issued by the ME, for example those related to safety of staff and patients, personal confidentiality and privacy.

FROM WHERE DOES A TRUST DERIVE ITS INCOME?

Prior to the NHS reforms, hospitals and units were allocated their income on an annual basis solely from their host District Health Authority (DHA). Since the reforms, a fundamental change has taken place. Trusts generate their income in two ways:

1. Trusts contract for the supply of services to their purchasers (commissioners), who may be what was the DHA, GP fund-holders and possibly Social Services and the private sector. Trusts may retain the surpluses from this activity and from the sale of assets such as land, buildings and equipment. This type of income – revenue – is intended to cover a Trust's running costs.

2. Capital items and projects are funded through a mechanism called the External Financing Limit (EFL). The EFL is explained in detail on page 21.

Subject to the approval of the Secretary of State, Trusts may borrow, from either the public or private sector, although the cost of borrowing from the latter is likely to be more expensive and so less attractive to, or permitted by, the Treasury. However, recent changes in the rules allowing inward investment into the NHS by the private sector mean that, where the business case can be justified, ' partnership' arrangements can be agreed, up to a limit of £10 million.

Ministers are currently encouraging Trusts to look for private sector funding for capital projects, before seeking funding from the centre. This partnership funding is likely to become a more common method of funding projects and developments.

It is important to bear in mind that, for the Secretary of State to guarantee the borrowing of a Trust from the private sector, distinct advantages must be demonstrated over borrowing from the Treasury. Trusts may borrow on an unguaranteed basis, only if they are able to demonstrate that it is cheaper than other forms of borrowing – a very rare scenario.

Before any borrowing may take place, a Trust must demonstrate that it is able to meet its commitments and pay the interest on the loan and repay it in full, within the agreed timescale.

The timing of loans is important. Trusts may only borrow money when they need it. It is not permitted for a Trust to borrow at low rates of interest and place the money on deposit to generate income. For day to day transactions and cash management purposes, however, Trusts may use interest earning bank accounts. This will be a new departure for many finance departments, set up as a result of achieving Trust status. So-called Treasury management policies should be in place, making it clear what the Trust's policies are in relation to investments, where the investments may be made, who has the authority to make the investment decisions and so on.

TRUSTS MAY NOT:

1. Use their assets as security for a loan or mortgage.

2. Borrow in foreign currencies – except with the permission of the Secretary of State.

3. Make speculative investments, such as in futures, options or interest rate swaps.

Investments

Trusts may invest in Government Securities, local authorities, nationalized industries, banks and building societies. Sorry, the Bahamas Branch of the International Bank of Glitter and Run Quick is out – however much interest they offer!

Accounts

Trusts must produce annual accounts based, fundamentally, on the requirements of the Companies Acts. The Trust's chief executive (not the director of finance) has the ultimate responsibility for ensuring, on behalf of the Board, that the accounts show a true and fair statement of the Trust's position and that standing financial instructions are complied with; all public funds have been managed properly and protected; and the accounts are properly presented. The chief executive, advised by the director of finance, is answerable on behalf of the Board, for any questions about a Trust's accounts and for informing the ME if the long-term viability of the Trust is at risk.

Trust funds

Donations and bequests, given to hospitals in the past, become the responsibility of the Trust Board acting as trustees. In some cases enormous funds can accumulate and sometimes special trustees are appointed to administer funds. The Trust funds may only be applied to the purposes for which they were donated and must be accounted for separately. They are quite separate from the day to day income of the Trust.

Tax

Trusts pay no tax in the ordinary sense, such as capital gains tax etc. However, they are responsible for payments of income tax and national insurance contributions on behalf of their staff – just like any other business. Trusts are also responsible for making super-annuation payments on behalf of employees.

Insurance

Trusts should make arrangements to cover all risks other than those arising from clinical negligence. Claims for clinical negligence are currently met from within the external financing limit (EFL). This is of particular concern for Trusts working in high risk areas such as maternity and sensitive surgical disciplines. The increasing willingness on the part of patients to engage in litigation is a matter for concern and some modification of the current arrangements is under discussion.

Ownership of assets

Trusts own their own assets which are transferred to them from the DHA following negotiation but they may only take into ownership those assets they need for their activities. There is no obligation for a Trust to take on assets and a Trust may wish to negotiate with the DHA for a leasehold interest in certain assets. Trusts are free to dispose of assets up to the value of £1 million. Over this sum the approval of the Secretary of State is required. All disposals must be included in the annual business plan.

Staff

Trusts are free to employ all staff directly (including clinicians), on local terms and conditions. Trusts are responsible for their own industrial relations and personnel matters.

Supplies

Trusts are free to purchase supplies and services from wherever they consider is best value for money. There is a general obligation on Trusts to achieve best value for money in all matters.

4

Glossary of Terms

Originating assets

Each Trust owns its assets, that is to say its land, buildings and equipment. The assets are valued and added together. The total is called the originating asset. The value of these assets is regarded by the Treasury as a 'debt' because the transfer of the asset to the Trust takes place without payment. The asset becomes the Capital Debt owed to the Treasury. The valuation of assets is undertaken by the district valuer, at the assets' open market value for their existing use. Where land and buildings become surplus to requirements, they are revalued at their open market value for an alternative use.

Capital debt

The capital debt is split into two elements: interest bearing debt and public dividend capital. The balance of the split between the two elements is agreed by the Secretary of State with the Treasury, individually for each Trust, as part of the application to achieve Trust status. Commonly, the split is fifty:fifty—half interest bearing debt and half public dividend capital.

Interest bearing debt (IBD)

That part of the original capital debt on which the Trust will be obliged to repay interest to the Treasury. The repayments, including interest, will be made over a defined period, usually related to the life of the assets of the Trust, and in general for a period that does not exceed 20 years.

The repayments may be by way of: annual payments, where the principal is repaid in equal amounts each year, with interest calculated on a reducing balance; on an annuity basis, where the same payment is made each year but the proportion of principal and interest is modified as the debt is repaid; on a term basis, where the principal is repaid at the end of the period and interest is paid during the life of the loan.

A Trust may apply to pay off IBD early and it may be possible to negotiate a discount for early payment.

Public dividend capital (PDC)

In practice Trusts pay no return (dividend) on their PDC. The PDC is held by the Treasury. There is no regular schedule of return and no short-term obligation. When Trusts have fulfilled their fixed interest obligations (the IBD) and a surplus exists, the Treasury may require a repayment of part of the PDC. This is a possibility when a Trust disposes of an asset such as the sale of land.

External financing limit (EFL)

The EFL seems to cause more confusion than any other factor and is the phrase most people have the greatest problem in defining and explaining. Let's try!

The EFL is, in effect, a cash limit and is the difference between the amount of money generated in the Trust and the total amount it needs to carry out its plans. In effect, how much 'external' money the Trust needs. It is not intended to cover running costs, but one off costs such as capital. An EFL may be 'positive' or 'negative'.

A positive EFL is where the Trust wishes to spend more money than it is able to generate for itself and needs to borrow, externally, to fund its proposed programme.

A negative EFL is where the Trust will generate more money than it needs to fund its plans. Some of the balance may be used to repay loans, or may be invested. Where the money is invested, the investment will be held by the Trust and used to support future spending.

An EFL of zero simply means spending and income are equal.

5

What Information does the Board Need?

Sometimes, rather confusingly called 'management information', this is the specific information that the Board will have on a regular basis, which will be used as the yardstick by which the Board can measure the progress of the organization.

The strategic direction

All Trusts are required to produce a strategic direction document. The aim is to examine the long-term strategy of the organization, for the purposes of both clarifying the thinking of the organization and to enable the Management Executive of the Department of Health to take a wider view of health provision and development throughout the country as a whole.

The business plan

PREPARATION

Great emphasis is placed on Trusts' business plans. Each Trust is required to produce an annual business plan for the year ahead and for two more forward years. Business plans from individual Trusts form part of the overview of health delivery throughout the UK and are used by the Department of Health when judging what to bid for in its negotiations with the Treasury and to gauge the likely public expenditure requirement. The business plan is the most important document in the organization and it is the Board's job to ensure it is prepared properly and carried through. It is also essential that the business plan links with the purchaser's planning cycle.

A business plan is not a Polaroid photograph of the future, a forecast or glimpse into the tea leaves. A business plan is not designed to be slavishly followed line by line, figure by figure.

A business plan is about assembling the best information you can *today*, to enable you to make reliable decisions about *tomorrow*. Trusts will want to prepare a business plan when they start out as a Trust; to prepare for the next financial year; when they see a change in direction; and as part of the ongoing process of reviewing progress and direction.

Business plans are important whatever the type of Trust. The changing pace of medical technology places less and less reliance on the old style 4–500 bed acute general hospital, and creates more and more opportunities for treatment and services to be delivered in community style facilities.

The results of research, teaching and development will most likely mean centres of excellence developing away from the city centre teaching hospitals. The break up of the old style institution for the mentally ill, results in providing services of a very different type. Every Trust is involved in some form of radical change. If not today then at some time in the future they will all be faced with some difficult decisions about the future of their 'business'. The business plan is a vital part of planning today for what needs to be done tomorrow.

Guidelines for the format of the business plan are provided by the ME and the timescale for compiling and submitting the plan is also prescribed by the ME.

Major capital schemes will require additional planning. These plans are called 'Business Cases'. These documents address issues of funding, where the money will come from and whether the target rate of return can be achieved. How will the scheme be supported in the future; is there purchaser support for what is being planned; and will they place contracts? An option appraisal will be required and the scheme justified against the most rigorous and thoughtful planning. A business case document for a major capital scheme is often produced 'out of house' by external business consultants. Producing a business case can consume hours of management time. The final document should be approved by the Board.

There are three fundamental elements to a business plan:

- agreeing what the objectives are

- planning what needs to be done to achieve the objectives

- ensuring the funds are available to carry out the plans.

Objectives

A Trust will need to be sure what its objectives are. To open a new orthopaedic ward is not an objective. To get enough business to make opening a new orthopaedic ward worthwhile and enable it to stay open is an objective!

Planning

Rudyard Kipling spoke of 'his friends, good and true: How, What, Why, When and Who'. The business planner would do well to recruit Kipling's friends. *How* do we know we need a new orthopaedic department; *What* will it do; *Why* do we need to do it; *When* is it needed and *Who* will use it and work in it?

The Board will want satisfactory answers for Rudyard Kipling's friends – and a lot more beside! Identifying specific sources for contract income, staff, building programmes and developments will need specific and realistic timetables for achievement. Be prepared for the plans to go wrong (they often do) or be delayed (they always are), and think about contingencies.

6

Budgets and Funding

Budgets will be the province of the finance director, who will prepare the Trust's budgets after consultation with budget holders and managers. Members of the Board must be sure that the budgets are 'owned' by the organization and not dumped on managers from on high! The temptation is for budgets to be prepared by the finance folk and handed out like tablets of stone to Moses.

However tight the organization is for cash, it is vital for the success of budget planning that managers are fully aware of what is expected of them.

The Management Executive of the Department of Health has three main financial requirements for Trusts. Trust Boards are responsible for ensuring:

1. They achieve the *target rate of return*. This is a real 'pre-interest' return of 6% on the value of net assets. Net assets means an average of assets owned at the beginning of the year and those owned at the end of the year. This allows for disposals and acquisitions during the year.

2. They *break-even* on income and expenditure after taking into
    account repayments of loans and interest bearing debt (IBD),
    taking one year with another. An over-run in one year must be
    compensated for the next. During the year a Trust may use an
    overdraft facility to tide over short-term deficits, but they must
    be repaid and the books balanced by the end of the year.

3. They work within their *external financing limit* (EFL). Some
    facility exists in that a Trust may borrow, in the last quarter of
    the year, (with the ME's consent) extra funding of about 1% of
    the sum of its total turnover and expenditure of fixed assets.
    Beware, the borrowing will be deducted from next year's EFL!

It is against this background that Trusts operate and must plan their
budgets. The business plan must ensure that the three main requirements are fulfilled along with the aims of the organization.

Putting the budget together

Budgets are signposts for the future and the benchmarks against
which the Board can measure progress. Fundamentally, a budget
should aim at providing:

- a balance sheet

- an overall profit and loss account

- a cash-flow forecast.

Budgets should also:

- Contain income and expenditure budgets based on activity, manpower and finance.

- Comprise the business plans of the business managers in the various departments and functions of the Trust.

- Be prepared, ready for use at the beginning of the financial year. In the case of NHS Trusts, this means April. The temptation may be to wait for the outcome of the previous year and build on a known outcome. This will not do. Without a budget at the beginning of the year, it will be impossible to measure the performance of the organization as the year progresses.

- Separate out discrete activity (Functions) and provide information for monitoring activity, manpower and finance.

- Be produced regularly, to identify trends. For example; if the results of departmental activity are presented to the Board monthly, the format should remain monthly. To increase or decrease the timescale would distort the results and make comparisons worthless.

- Be detailed enough to be interesting and helpful, but not be so detailed as to be confusing. There are so many ways in which modern computer technology has made the presentation of really complex information easy and simple to understand. Software is cheap and misunderstandings are expensive. Be sure to invest in the right information technology. Computer graphics, graphs, pie charts and bar charts all help to make comparisons with 'last month and budget' simple. The impact of a graphic presentation of numbers and figures should not be underestimated. Even seasoned finance people agree, a picture is worth a thousand sums! A Board director will be doing the organization a big favour by asking for a graphical portrayal of the financial performance and comparisons of a department.

• Not be a substitute for getting close to the 'business' and picking up comments such as, 'We got through this month OK, but we've got a real tough month coming and we could over-spend'!

How should a budget be prepared?

Each department should be isolated and asked what its activity will be for the year ahead. The simple trap that many 'budget setters' fall into is to take last year's outcome and add a bit on for this year. The right way to prepare a budget is to start afresh with each year. This is called 'zero based budgeting'. Zero basing means starting with a blank sheet of paper for each year. For a Trust that has been in 'business' for more than a year (and in many cases for a new Trust) the past is seen as the best guide for the future. However, this approach can reproduce the mistakes of the past and compound their errors. Zero based budgeting is the ideal and should be aimed for wherever possible.

Changing the budget

In the real world, the performance of the organization is unlikely to be a mirror image of the budget. Indeed, be suspicious if it is! The purpose of the budget is to highlight deviations from it. Some people regard the budget as a benchmark and this is a good way to look at it. Do not panic when deviations occur. Ask for a reason and consider the answer against what you know about the business of the Trust and your 'feel' for what is going on.

Ask questions. The director needs to consider whether the variations are a result of the poor performance of the organization, or the budget was wrong in the first place. If fundamental errors are apparent in the budget then a revision may be needed. There should also be some questions asked about the veracity of the planning process that produced the budget in the first place.

Check list

There are four fundamentals to cover when preparing a business plan:

1. Be sure the assumptions that are made in the plan about the level of trading stand up to the most rigorous testing. Are they realistic? Will purchasers keep buying what you are offering and how can you be sure?

2. What is the impact of inflation likely to be? It is easy to think inflation is off the agenda – beware, it never is.

3. If the business plan contains plans for capital developments, be 100 per cent sure that the funding plans are in place and there is the assurance of sufficient business (revenue) to keep them going. Avoid speculative assumptions.

4. Test all assumptions to destruction! The professionals call it sensitivity analysis. In everyday language it means: make sure you have asked a lot of questions that start with the phrase 'What if . . .' A risk analysis to deal with unforeseen variations in income or expenditure is a vital component in the planning process to introduce some flexibility into the budgeting process.

WHEN THE BUSINESS PLAN IS FINISHED HOW WILL IT BE JUDGED?

There are eight basic tests which the business plan will have to pass.

1. The Trust must meet its financial obligations and duties. No one wants the embarrassment of a Trust going broke or not being able to honour its obligations.

2. Where capital developments are involved: is there enough money in the system to provide the income for the Trust to pay off its borrowings and run what is planned? This is a vital test sometimes called the test of affordability. In simple terms it means: notwithstanding the fact that your purchaser may be very keen to use the new service you are offering, and is prepared to 'sign up' for the new service, how can you be sure that there will be enough money in the system for the purchasers to meet their obligations to you. In other words, can they afford it?

3. Does the business plan fit in with the Trust's own strategy and direction and with the regional and district strategy for health care? From this it will be obvious that business planning cannot

be carried out in a vacuum. The Trust must be aware of what is going on around them. There is a purpose in planning to build a long-stay institution for the mentally ill if the region has decided to close long-stay institutions!

4. The business plan must demonstrate that there is control over the working capital in the 'business'.

5. Where borrowing is undertaken and investments are to be made, strategies should have been thought through and plans should be sensible and achievable.

6. There should be sufficient cash in the 'business' to make repayments of interest bearing debt.

7. If the Trust is to depend on income from non-NHS sources, such as a private wing to a hospital, is the income to be relied upon or is it speculative? To what extent would the Trust be at risk if the plans failed to materialize?

8. What is the sensitivity of the key assumptions made in the plan? Are they realistic?

As time goes by and the Trust's plans unfold, a comparison of what was planned and what actually happened will be made. Appraisal is an ongoing process; just because the plan is made and underway, it is not forgotten! Close monitoring will take place, to ensure the Trust is living up to its promises!

When budgets are agreed, what next?

As the year progresses, directors will wish to ensure that the organization is living up to expectations. A management reporting system is required.

Reporting systems

If the business plan is the map for the journey to be undertaken by the Trust in the year ahead, then the management reports mark the 'X' on the map to show how the journey has progressed and where you are!

SIX BASIC QUESTIONS A DIRECTOR WILL NEED ANSWERS TO

1. *How is each part of the business doing?*

   In compiling the business plan, each department of the Trust is asked to go back to square one and predict, on the best information available, what they could be expected to achieve and contribute to the overall success of the organization in the year ahead. The director will need to know if their aims are 'going to plan', and if not what help they need, or what other action needs to be taken to ensure they will perform.

2. *What is the overall position of the organization?*

   This can be drawn together from the information from each of the budget holding departments. Will the aims and plans of the business as a whole be achieved? If there are signs of slippage or failure, what action needs to be taken?

3. *How is the Trust performing against contracts?*

   Are block contracts being completed too slowly or too quickly? Will the organization run out of work before the end of the year? Is this planned for? Will there be a public relations problem, or even a question of redundancy? Can more work be obtained? If cost and volume contracts are being undertaken, the same questions will apply. In cost per case contracts, are the original costings holding up, are they accurate? Conversely, is the organization doing too much work; exceeding contract and expectations and, in the language of business, 'over-trading'.

4. *Is the income of the Trust reaching expectations?*

   This means, are the customers paying their bills on time? Contracted income is usually easy to collect, but assume nothing. Payment for work outside contracts, such as extra contractual referrals (ECRs) needs to be watched too. For example, if a Trust is located near a busy motorway, accident and emergency admissions, which can have considerable financial consequences as a result of complicated treatments, are paid for through the ECR system. Directors will need to know that their Trust is getting paid. Similarly, if the Trust has a specialty that patients are referred to from all over the country, the collection of payment may be complex and involve a great deal of money – watch it!

5. *Is there enough cash in the business to support the current, and expected, levels of activity?*

   Monitoring the cash flow statement will be important. Look for trends. Is the Trust reducing its surplus, is there a trend?

6. *Is the Trust paying its debts?*

The easiest way for an organization to fool itself into a false sense of security is not to pay anyone and use other people's money. Old style District Health Authorities were renowned for stretching their creditors and carrying forward a huge bow-wave of debt from year to year. Trusts are obliged to pay their creditors within an eight week cycle and may only carry forward debt in exceptional circumstances – times are changing!

To answer these questions make sure:

1. The Board agrees on the information it wants and how it should be presented. Does everyone understand the reports? Remember that executive directors are not all expected to be financial geniuses and non-executives may not be specialists in finance. If you do not understand something, say so! You are responsible for the organization. Do not think for one moment that the Trust's auditors or the public accounts committee will accept the excuse 'I'm sorry, I didn't understand!'

2. Ensure that the timetable for reporting is agreed and stuck to. Do not accept the excuse: information was not available because there was not enough time. Insist, get tough, make a fuss, but get the information to the Board on time. Timeliness is more important that micrometer accuracy.

When should the information be available?

If the Board has decided to meet monthly, then the information should be available for the Board meeting. It is important that the information is accurate and timeliness should not be sacrificed for accuracy. However, modern computing makes the keeping of records and the analysis of information easy. Many Trusts are able to produce a statement of their cash position on a daily basis and some even boast about being able to provide a daily mini-balance sheet. Most companies in the private sector have been doing this for years!

Seven golden rules

There is no point in having information if it does not mean anything to the director reading it!

1. Current information should be compared with the business plan and the budget. Is the organization doing what it said it would do and is it doing it when it said it would? Also, is it doing what it is supposed to do in the way that it promised it would? Remember Rudyard Kipling's friends? They will stand you in good stead!

2. Is the information presented in a way that is understandable to you and the rest of the Board? Make absolutely sure you understand what is going on. If there is a doubt in your mind – express it. The chances are that the rest of the Board will be struggling to understand that the information too, but are too shy to say so!

3. Is the information about the performance of the organization being consistently compared over the same period of time? If the information is supposed to be monthly, make sure it stays on a monthly cycle. There is no point in comparing apples with oranges, or apples with light bulbs! If budgets are to be compared monthly, make sure the report is monthly and kick up a stink if it is not.

4. Make sure that the staff are involved in the budget process. Ensure that the coal-face knows how much coal it is supposed to dig and agrees it can deliver. Imposing budgets on staff is the kind of macho management everyone can do without. If the money situation is tight, share this knowledge with the staff. The chances are that they will understand and help you through a difficult patch. 'Devolve' a budget onto them and they will probably screw you up – and a good job too. The staff are the Trust's most important asset. Get them on board, with the Board.

5. Insist that budgets are prepared for the year, before the beginning of the year. Do not accept a budget that is cobbled together after the start of the financial year. The benchmarks must be put in place before the beginning of the year.

6. Do not accept the assumption that the budget will be the same as last year. I give you the absolute guarantee that it will not be.

7. Do not get bogged down in unnecessary complications. There is a temptation for budget holders to shuffle off their costs to another department. Look out for shared costs, recharges and internal cost centres. Wherever the costs come from, it is still part of the same organization. Departmental costs, charges and

nominal entries for repairs, maintenance and services are all indicators that are worth a second look. The first rule is to 'keep it simple'.

A word or two about cash

First word: No matter how elegant the plans, if the cash runs out you are in trouble.

Second word: Cash can run out if you do too much work (known as over-trading), and the cash can run out if you do too little work. Ask the question: is activity matching the forecast, the business plan and gut feeling?

What of the future?

Trusts are required to produce 'strategic plans'. They are the long-term strategy of the Trust, its ambitions and vision of the future. They should be the natural consequence of the business planning process.

Where is the Trust going and how will it get there?

Plans to develop services are just pie in the sky if they do not secure the long-term support of the purchasers. Are the Trust's plans linked to the forward plan of the purchaser? What is the element of risk? What is the gap between the cost of the operation and the known income?

Ask the questions. If the answer is, 'Well there is a shortfall of income over costs, but by the time the service (or whatever) comes on stream we think we will be able to fund the deficit', be ruthless. Your instinct must be to say NO! Risks do pay off sometimes and the director should be prepared to take risks. *But*, be sure you understand and you know what you are getting into. If there is doubt, insist on a third party evaluation of what is being proposed.

Capital projects need a very close examination. The current trend is for 'down-sizing' services. Medical technology has put the NHS in a difficult position. The local hospital, for which a local population can have such an understandable affection, is unlikely to be needed in its present form, over the next ten years. Day case procedures, hospital at home initiatives, community services and GP fundholders are all developing and the result will be a very different NHS. Beware, in the words of the sixties song: 'times are a changing'. Before committing the Trust to a capital development, ask the question and insist on the answer: 'Is there purchaser support for this proposal?'

The Management Executive of the Department of Health will require the business case to be fully worked through and justified. The risks will have to be analysed along with the competitiveness of the prices to be charged for the service. Directors can expect a rigorous and exhaustive dissection of plans. Be patient, do not give up and, remember, you are spending taxpayers' money!

How can the Board measure its progress?

Keeping track of the progress of the organization is a frustrating task. Regular reports on the financial status of the organization can help, but there are other factors that a director will wish to consider. Each Trust is independent and each Trust will face a set of issues that are particular to its progress and situation. Knowing what questions to ask is an important part of getting the right answers! There are a number of 'quick comparators' that a director might suggest as a quick acid test of performance.

The comparators are not definitive but do have a relevance. They may well point the way to other benchmarks that can be tailored to the specific needs of your Trust. Use the results with caution and as a tool to detect trends.

7

Questions to Ask

Getting the right answers depends on asking the right questions. What to ask can be a problem for a new director. There is no list of definitive questions, so much will depend on the individual Trust. Also, it is important that the Board works as a team and Board meetings do not turn into a judge and jury session.

Here are some questions that directors might like to ask, to get a feel for how the organization is doing.

Quality

In acute services it may be useful to know how well the clinicians are performing. How often do they have to do the job again, how often do they not get it right first time? Mistakes can be costly.

Get a feel for how many unplanned readmissions there are less than one month after discharge.

The same sort of question can be applied to unplanned returns to theatre. In the language of business, how often does the job have to be done again?

Customer complaints

Complaints are a good way of assessing the effectiveness of the organization. In any large organization there will be complaints. Indeed it is no disgrace to get some complaints (provided there are not too many); the measure of the organization is how well and quickly things that are wrong are put right and how the organization can demonstrate that it has learned from the experience. Ask about complaints. The number of complaints can be an unreliable indicator. Find out the average time (in days) for a complaint to be resolved.

Also ask about compliments. How many do you get? Make sure you give a pat on the back too!

Occupancy rate

How fast the throughput of the hospital is, is becoming a very important issue. Patient stays should, of course, be long enough to ensure that treatment is appropriate and thorough. That said, it is of vital importance that there is a measure of the efficiency of the organization in using its assets. Try dividing the total number of in-patient days by the number of in-patient beds in service. Keep track of the figure over six months and see if there is a trend developing.

Watch out for declining occupancy rates; this will raise questions about down-sizing, over-activity and the use of capacity.

Use of capital items

Take operating theatres as an example. Compare the number of hours the theatres could be used against the number of hours they *are* being used. Include evenings and weekends! Think about capital items as money eating monsters and you may turn them into money making monsters.

Look out for low utilization; it can reveal poor management, scheduling problems, and the need to scale down capacity.

Inventory

This may be a difficult comparator to get the data for. However, it is worth doing. The idea is to get a feel for how well the organization is handling assets, whether the inventory levels are high and the effectiveness of asset management. A neat trick is to divide the total value of the organization's inventory at month end, by the number of in-patient beds in service!

Human resources

Seventy per cent plus of the organization's revenue budget will be spent on staff. Staff are the most valuable asset in a service industry – and that is exactly what the NHS is. Ask about the numbers of staff leaving, is there a trend? Ask about the numbers off sick. Do the 'leavers and sickers' all come from the same part of the organization? Is there a management or morale problem? Try these comparators, to get a feel for how you are doing.

High leaving statistics can point to problems. The cost of recruiting and training staff is high. Low staff turnover is always better than high numbers of staff leaving. Why are staff leaving? Pay, child-minding facilities, travel to work, security, training and a host of issues can be revealed by keeping a watch on this comparator.

Also, the number of accidents suffered by staff can give a feel for training needs (if the accident list is full of staff absent because of backache, is lifting a problem?).

Questions and comparisons, used month on month, can give a feel for how the organization is running. It is important that the Board does not try to manage the organization, but comparators will reassure the Board that the organization is being run properly. There is nothing worse for a Board, than to be faced by a crisis that they could have seen coming. Using the right tools to measure the organization month on month is a way of spotting problems on the horizon.

8

Governance

Corporate governance is at the heart of the fulfilment of a director's duties in the public arena. How the Board retains full and effective control over the organization and monitors the executive process is a fundamental question to address.

The Cadbury Report

The enquiry into the financial aspects of corporate governance, under the chairmanship of Sir Adrian Cadbury, took 18 months to sift evidence and shape the so-called 'Cadbury Report', published in December 1992.

The report was occasioned by the events surrounding the demise of BCCI, the Maxwell scandals and the heightened public concerns over the pay rises some public company chairmen were seen to have awarded themselves.

'Cadbury' produced draft proposals that have been widely accepted as a way forward for the conduct of public company business.

The House of Commons Public Accounts Committee expressed concerns about the issues of corporate governance in the public sector. The NHS and the NHS reforms, and issues surrounding some Regional Health Authorities and other organizations in healthcare, have made the Health Service particularly vulnerable, and indeed the Department of Health Management Executive has published guidance on the matter.

The relevance of the Cadbury Report to health and the NHS is obvious. As more and more NHS units move towards achieving self-governing status, so the need to demonstrate impartiality and probity in the decisions and activities of NHS Trusts increases.

The full implications of the Cadbury Report are for the private sector and public companies generally. However, because Trusts are responsible for public money (in some cases a great deal of public money), it is a wise Board that will choose to embrace the recommendations of Cadbury to the fullest extent. There is nothing to fear in doing so and a great deal to be gained.

THE MAIN SECTIONS OF THE CADBURY REPORT COVER:

1. The Board

2. Non-executive directors

3. Executive directors

4. Reporting and controls.

Let us examine the report and put it into the appropriate context for health and NHS Trusts. 'Cadbury' recommends:

THE BOARD SHOULD

1. *Meet regularly.*

   There are no legal and specific requirements to oblige Trust
   Boards to meet more than once a year in public. The question of
   the frequency of Board meetings is covered elsewhere in this
   book. Suffice to say, at this point, that directors should satisfy
   themselves that the Board is meeting frequently enough to
   ensure that the organization is being properly run and is meeting
   the planned targets set by the Board.

2. *Retain full and effective control over the company and monitor
   the executive management.*

   Here issues of compliance and other factors come into play. In
   general terms it means that a Board needs to put in place
   mechanisms, checks and balances that ensure that the business
   of the organization is being conducted properly and that there
   are unlikely to be too many unpleasant surprises sprung on the
   Board.

3. *Clearly accepted division of responsibility at the head of the
   'company' (in the case of the NHS substitute the word Trust). No
   one is to have unfettered powers of decision.*

   Financial standing orders and standing financial instructions are
   issued to Trusts on achieving Trust status. At the first meeting
   of the Board, on becoming a Trust, the Board will be asked to
   adopt the standing orders and standing financial instructions.
   How goods and services are tendered for will be dealt with in
   those documents. Other factors, such as the chairman's action
   between meetings and powers to act outside the boardroom are

for the Board to agree on and record in the minutes of the Board meeting.

4. *Have non-executive directors of sufficient calibre and numbers for their views to carry weight.*

    This is a Cadbury recommendation that is easy for the Board to comply with. Legislation requires that NHS Trust Boards have five non-executive directors, five executive directors and a chairman. In the case of a smaller Trust the numbers can be reduced to four – both for non-executive and executive directors.

    The executive directors (except in the case of Ambulance Trusts) must include: a chief executive, a medical director, a nurse director, a finance director and one other. Boards may appoint associate directors of such numbers as they think fit. However, the associate directors may not vote on any item before the Board.

5. *Establish a formal schedule of matters reserved for the Board, for decisions to ensure direction and for control to be firmly in the Board's hands.*

    The schedule of matters specifically reserved for the attention of the Board should be spelled out. The schedule should at least cover:

    a) Acquisition and disposal of assets.

    b) Investments.

    c) Capital projects.

    d) Authority levels and delegated powers.

e) Treasury (or finance) policies.

f) Risk management policies.

g) Procedures for action between board meetings.

h) Signatories for transactions.

These procedures should be laid down formally by resolution of the Board and included in the appointment letters of those concerned.

In addition, the monitoring of the business plan is a matter for the Board to consider regularly.

6. *Agree procedures for the directors to take independent advice if necessary and at the company's expense.*

This 'Cadbury' recommendation is primarily aimed at private sector companies in the throes of takeover or acquisition battles. Directors opposing recommendations to the Board may wish for the help of some independent advice before arriving at a decision. In the case of the NHS Trust, it will be common that the Board as a whole will look to outside consultants for advice. However, there may come a time when the Board is undecided, or split over a proposal or course of action. Board directors should be in a position to seek independent, outside advice if it will help them evaluate a proposal and make an informed decision. This may well have resource implications; advice will need to be paid for. Nevertheless, if directors are to be able to exercise their functions properly (particularly non-executive directors) it is important that their decisions are informed.

Non-executive directors should

1. *Bring independent judgement to bear on issues of strategy, performance, resources, including key appointments and standards of conduct.*

   Non-executive directors will be selected for their independence of mind, their knowledge of the community or a specific skill. The key word is independence. Their overview of strategy and monitoring the performance of the organization will be the key to the success of their Trust. Maintaining the balance between independence and involvement with the organization, using their skills and monitoring performance will not be easy for everyone at first.

2. *Be independent of management and free from any business or other relationship which could materially interfere with the exercise of judgement. Their fee should reflect the time which they commit to the 'company'.*

   In our case the word 'company' means Trust. Pay scales for non-executives are established by the Department of Health, are linked to Civil Service pay scales and 'banded' to reflect the revenue budget of the Trust. They are reviewed most years, generally in line with inflation. The pay scale for the non-executive is not a matter for the Board to decide. The question of freedom from business and other interests is a matter that the Board must take very seriously. Over time it is likely that a national register of interests will be kept by the Department of Health. Scrupulous standards are required in the public sector and the Board would do well to establish its own register of members' interests.

3. *Be appointed for a specific term and reappointment should not be automatic.*

    Non-executive directors are appointed for either a two- or four-year term of office. This is a matter decided by the Department of Health. There is a tendency to appoint more two-year posts than four-year posts.

    Whilst it is accepted that a continuation of membership can bring stability and continuity to the work of the Board, reappointment is by no means automatic. The chairman should prepare a good case for the reappointment of a non-executive director and also have given thought to succession planning in the event of a reappointment not being made or a member wishing to stand down.

4. *Be selected through a formal process and their appointment should be a matter for the Board as a whole.*

    Selection to the Board is a matter for the Secretary of State. Chairmen will be asked to make recommendations, generally of more than one candidate. Current national policy is to increase the opportunities for women to become members of Boards.

    If a Board is to be regarded as a team, then it seems reasonable that the chairman should have a considerable say in who should be in that team. However, a chairman must be in a position to demonstrate that due regard has been given to:

    a) the balance of male and female members of the Board

    b) reflecting in Board membership the ethnic origin of the catchment area the Trust is serving

c) the value of the skills and experience of the members brought to the work of the organization

d) impartiality in the selection process.

Executive directors should

1. *Not have service contracts exceeding three years, without share-holders' approval.*

   Adoption of this 'Cadbury' recommendation would cause some managers to have a heart attack! The NHS is often thought of as a 'job for life'. The opportunities open to Trusts, as a result of the NHS reforms, mean that short-term contracts for senior managers and directors could become the order of the day. Indeed, in many Trusts, short-term, rolling contracts are starting to become established. Performance targets, performance management, everywhere the word is performance. For the director who can 'perform' there is nothing to fear – and a good deal to be gained. For the others – watch out!

2. *Disclose total emoluments, including: chairman, highest paid UK director (including stock options and pension contributions). Separate figures for performance related elements and on what basis the performance is measured should be provided.*

   Trust annual returns are required to follow present company policy and declare the salary of the highest paid director. In the USA, following the Treadway Report (their equivalent to our Cadbury Report), greater emphasis is being given to declaring all aspects of emoluments, including the formulae for calculating performance pay and the salaries of other directors. In the NHS we are dealing with more than just the shareholders' cash. In the NHS the shareholder is the Nation and Boards may consider a greater openness is good for the image of the organization. Indeed, over time, it could become a requirement.

3. *Have their pay determined by a remunerations committee, composed mainly or wholly of non-executive directors.*

   The concept of a remuneration committee may be new to healthcare. However, the concept of outside consultants evaluating the pay of senior staff is not.

   Remuneration committees can undertake the task, with the help of outside consultants. The committee should be comprised exclusively of non-executive directors. The USA Treadway Report recommends that the names of the members of the remunerations committee are shown in the annual report and the members of the committee should be available to answer questions at the annual general meeting. Boards may like to get used to the practice now – before it becomes obligatory!

Reporting and controls

1. *It is the Board's duty to report a balanced assessment of the 'company's' position.*

   The annual report is the place where the Board reports on the activity of the Trust over the preceding year. Currently most returns contain a report from the chairman and another from the chief executive and what amounts to a synopsis of the business plan, to date. The reports must be a fair reflection of the status of the organization, good points as well as bad. In addition the

Trust's accounts are presented, along with a certificate from the auditors that the facts and figures are a true and fair representation of the financial standing of the Trust. This type of reporting mirrors current practice in the private sector. In the future, best practice in the private sector may also require a statement from the directors that the report is a true and fair reflection of the company's activities and that the statements made and assessment given are accurate. This is a further 'certificate' of accuracy, over and above the opinion given by the auditors. Trust Boards may like to prepare today for changes that may come tomorrow.

2. *Ensure an objective and professional relationship with the auditors.*

Trusts are required to appoint auditors, who produce the impartial audit for the annual report.

Auditors also carry out a non-financial audit on certain management functions decided by the Management Executive of the Department of Health. In addition they are also able to carry out an audit of management functions at the request of the Board.

It is worth developing a good relationship with the auditors, not just at year end, but throughout the year. As the auditors gain a greater understanding of the Trust and the challenges it may face, so the process of audit becomes easier and quicker.

3. *Establish an audit committee of at least three non-executives, with written terms of reference and specific authority and duties.*

The concept of an audit committee is new to healthcare, although some Trusts do have them in place. They should be formally constituted and a model constitution for an audit committee is included in Appendix 1 of this book.

9

Additional Recommendations and Compliance

Directors have the ultimate responsibility for the conduct of their organizations. It is they and they alone, who carry the can if something goes wrong. The recommendations below are mainly common sense and are designed to provide a framework for peace of mind! The recommendations are not exhaustive, but will put the Board on the right road to achieving proper compliance with financial standing orders and governance, and, most important of all, an efficient working environment.

1. Sub-committees of the Board should comprise at least three non-executives – one of whom may be the chairman. This means that no one member of the Board has unfettered powers of decision.

2. The schedule of matters reserved for the Board should be given to all directors, on appointment, and kept up-to-date.

3. The Board should decide, in particular cases, whether or not its definition of independence is met.

4. Non-executives should not participate in performance or bonus schemes, neither should they be 'pensionable'.

5. Non-executives should have a clear letter of appointment; spelling out duties, terms of office, remuneration and its review.

6. A nomination committee should carry out the selection process and make proposals to the Board; composed mainly of non-executive directors.

7. The annual report should deal with setbacks as well as successes.

8. Audit committees

   a) Formal sub-committee of the main Board; written terms of reference; meet regularly (at least twice a year).

   b) Minimum of three members, all non-executives.

   c) External and internal auditors should attend the meetings. Other Board members have the right to attend.

   d) Audit committee, without executive members, to meet the external auditors at least once a year.

   e) Membership of the committee should be included in the annual report and the chairman of the committee be available to take questions at the annual general meeting.

9. Directors' responsibilities

   a) Prepare a financial statement each year, giving a true record of the company's position.

   b) Maintain true and accurate accounting records to safeguard assets, prevent fraud and irregularities.

   c) Confirm suitable accounting policies are in place and consistently applied.

   d) Confirm that applicable accounting standards have been followed; material departures noted in the annual report; such information made in statement immediately before the auditors' report.

10. Prepare a register of financial interests

   Some Board members may be selected specifically for their professional expertise and the skills they can bring to the Board.

   It is important that both the organization and the individuals are protected from a charge of exploitation of personal or private interests. A register of interests should be kept by the chief executive and the register regularly updated as members move on or their interests change. The register should be in the form of a book that is open to public inspection.

   The register should include such factors as:

   a) The professional occupation of members.

   b) Their dealings with the health service in their professional capacities.

c) Any personal interest or that of a close relative that could conflict with the impartiality of the member.

d) The acceptance of any hospitality or gift from any outside organization seeking to do business with the Trust.

e) The ownership of any shares in any company with which the Trust may do or seek to do business with.

f) Any involvement with any public body with which the Trust may seek commercial or other contact.

Members whose interests fall within the categories above, should ensure that their interests are registered in the book and withdraw from the proceedings of the Board if items are discussed that have a bearing on their interests. The fact that they have withdrawn should be noted in the minute book of the Board.

11. Ensure compliance with decisions and policy

Board debates, discussions and policy decisions are valueless unless the Board can be assured that they will be implemented. To ensure that the organization complies with the decisions of the Board, the following key questions should be asked. The answers to the questions will not always be a matter for the Board, but in the early days of a Trust, or when a new director joins a Trust, questions such as these are the legitimate territory of the member of a Board who will be ultimately responsible for the performance of the organization and the public money that is used to fund it.

a) Is there a clear written statement on how financial issues will be dealt with and who is responsible for making decisions at each level in the organization?

b) Has the Board voted to adopt model financial standing orders and are they in place?

c) Are there comprehensive standing financial instructions in place covering the full range of the Trust's financial activities?

d) Have clear policies been agreed for the appraisal of the investment of the Trust's funds and are there policies to cover: borrowing, treasury management, business planning, budgeting and reporting, selection and relationships with auditors?

e) How does the Board assure itself that financial instructions are being complied with? Where are the lines of responsibility and how are discrepancies reported and resolved?

f) Does the finance department have a business plan and what are its operational goals?

g) How does the finance department's business plan 'fit' with the organization's business plan?

h) Can the financial director assure the Board that there is an adequate structure within the finance department to monitor the performance of the department against the business plan?

i) Are the members of the finance department appropriately qualified?

j) Are there positive mechanisms in place to ensure that financial procedures are being complied with at every level – for example, capital investment through to bank reconciliations?

k) Is there an internal audit department, how does it interface with the audit committee, what are its reporting structures and is it adequately staffed by appropriately qualified people?

l) Can the Board be confident that the financial director is fully in touch with the working of their department and the financial position of the Trust?

m) Are financial reports to the Board accurate, timely and complete?

n) Is the finance department 'connected' with the organization; does it interface well with the business managers; does it respond to the business plan?

Appendix 1: Specimen Terms of Reference for an Audit Committee

Example for guidance only

Constitution

1. The Board hereby resolves to establish a Committee of the Board to be known as the Audit Committee.

Membership

2. The Committee shall be appointed by the Board from amongst the Non-Executive Directors of the Trust and shall consist of not fewer than three members. A quorum shall be two members.

3. The Chairman of the Committee shall be appointed by the Board.

Attendance at meetings

4. The Financial Director, the Head of Internal Audit, and a representative of the external auditors shall normally attend meetings. Other Board members shall also have the right of attendance. However, at least once a year the Committee shall meet with the external auditors without executive Board members present.

5. The Committee shall appoint a Secretary to the Committee. Cadbury describes this appointment as that of the Company Secretary. However, there is no similar post in a Trust. The appointment of the Financial Director as the Secretary may be considered as an alternative, but this may not be appropriate in all circumstances.)

Frequency of meetings

6. Meetings shall be held not less than twice a year. The external auditors may request a meeting if they consider that one is necessary.

Authority

7. The Committee is authorized by the Board to investigate any activity within its terms of reference. It is authorized to seek any information it requires from any employee and all employees are directed to co-operate with any reasonable request made by the Committee.

8. The Committee is authorized by the Board to obtain outside legal or other independent professional advice and to secure the attendance of outsiders with relevant experience and expertise if it considers this necessary.

Duties

9. The duties of the Committee shall be:

   a) to liaise with the Department of Health in matters concerning the appointment of the external auditor, monitor value for money in respect of their fee, and make recommendations to the Board in the event of resignation or dismissal of the auditors

   b) to discuss with the external auditor before the audit commences the nature and scope of the audit, and ensure co-ordination where more than one audit firm is involved

   c) to review the half-year and annual financial statements before submission to the Board, focusing particularly on:

      i) any changes in accounting policies and practices

      ii) major judgemental areas

      iii) significant adjustments resulting from the audit

      iv) assumptions about the viability of the organization

      v) compliance with accounting standards

      vi) compliance with Department of Health and legal requirements

   d) to discuss problems and reservations arising from the interim and final audits, and any matters the auditor may wish to discuss (in absence of management where necessary)

   e) to review the external auditor's management letter and management's response

f) to review the company's statement on internal control systems prior to endorsement by the Board

g) where an internal audit function exists: to review the internal audit programme, ensure co-ordination between the internal and external auditors, and ensure that the internal audit function is adequately resourced and has appropriate standing within the Trust

h   to consider the major findings of internal investigations and management's response

i) to consider other topics, as defined by the Board.

Reporting procedures

10. The Secretary shall circulate the minutes of meetings of the Committee to all members of the Board.

Appendix 2: Directors' Information Check List

To be able to judge the progress of the organization, and know if it is achieving its objectives, the Board must have information. For the information to be of any use it must be timely, relevant and accurate.

What information does the Board need? Each Trust will have its own agenda and its own needs, but as a starting point the Board should consider the following list as a basis for developing its own reporting strategies.

Contract performance

Keeping in touch with contract performance means keeping in touch with the heart of the business. The figures should monitor how much work is being completed, against how much work is expected to be completed. Performance against contract can show if more work is being accomplished than was expected, or if the volume of work is less than was expected. Either way, the Board needs to have the answers. Less than anticipated activity will mean a shortage of income that could lead to closures. More work being done will overheat the finances of the Trust and it could run out of money which might lead to closures.

Beds in use

Beds are the asset measurement of the Trust. The higher the through-put, the more the Board needs to know the situation. Rushed throughput can give rise to quality problems, slow throughput can mean underperformance or poor management.

Length of stay

Over the last ten years average bed stays in acute hospitals have reduced from an average of ten days to 6.5. Fluctuations in length of stay are a vital monitor of the performance of the organization. Specialty by specialty, the Board should know how the bed asset is being managed. In geriatric wards look out for protraction of length of stay resulting from poor discharge arrangements with Social Services.

Asset utilization

Before the NHS reforms, assets were described as a 'free good'. This meant that whatever the cost of the asset, no measurement of return was expected. Since the reforms, NHS Trusts have been required to produce a 6% return on assets and to allow for depreciation of the assets, up to 12%. The costs of the depreciation and returns are reflected in the Trust's prices. How assets are utilized has become a vitally important question to ask. No Trust can afford to have assets that are not being used to the full. The cost, for example, of a modern operating theatre can be very high indeed. The full utilization of the asset will be vital if the investment costs are to be realized.

Energy and water utilization

Audit Commission reports have pointed to the enormous waste the NHS suffers in the areas of water waste and energy use. The Board may be interested to know how energy and water consumption could be reduced.

Question tolerance violations on deviations from the norm

Clearly it is not practical, or even desirable, for the Board to be engaged in the minutiae of running the business. Neither should it bog itself down with data if all is well. Devising a formula to identify deviations from expected performance will be part of the Board's agenda in the formative period and planning for the future. Whatever targets are set, over time, some deviations will occur. In the best of well-run businesses things will not go according to plan from time to time. When events fall short of expectations it is important not to overreact. A momentary blip in performance is not the end of the world. The important thing is to spot trends. A shortfall one month is not important, unless it is followed by similar results in subsequent months. Allow a tolerance and let the Board agree on what the deviations from agreed performance might be. Ensure that tolerances set in advance are regularly reviewed.

Staff profile

The largest slice of the revenue budget will be spent on staff. They will be the most valuable asset and the most costly. How grades are made up and how skills and ages fit with the aims of the organization will be important for the Board to understand. For example, an organization aiming for growth, with a high number of staff approaching retirement, has a problem. Similarly, an organization aiming to down-size but with a high proportion of highly qualified staff needs to know how the skill-mix in the organization fits with future plans. If the organization is preparing to expand, does it have the appropriate number of qualified staff to make the plans work?

Turnover

Staff who do not 'stick' cost money. A high turnover of staff will indicate problems in the organization. Why are staff leaving? What is the cost of replacement and what can be done about leavers?

Absence rates

Providing health care is a stressful business, particularly in the fields of mental health and intensive care. Does stress play its part in high absenteeism or are there other factors? Is management good enough to prevent absenteeism and is it sensitive enough to recognize a potential problem? Is absenteeism confined to particular departments and what can the Board deduce from this?

Unit labour costs

This is a ratio that is in common use in the private sector as a measurement of costs. Unit labour costs are not often seen in the NHS. The calculation of the unit labour cost for departments as well as for the organization as a whole is an important financial measure. An increase in unit labour costs may point to increases in overtime payments or too high a grade of staff being unexpectedly employed. It is one of the most useful measures to cross the disciplines of the human resource department and the finance department and cannot be produced unless the two departments are working together.

Staff views/surveys

What staff feel about the organization is important. Regular surveys on such items as security, childcare facilities and a host of other matters will reveal problems on the horizon that can be dealt with before they become major issues.

Waiting list profiles

Who is waiting for what and for how long is useful for the Board to know. A growing waiting list for a particular specialty can point to a number of problems: poor management of resources, poor functioning medics, or a genuine and unforeseen swell in demand. The Board may wish management to act, or to talk to purchasers about their contracts.

Complaints/compliments

The reasons for this report are obvious. It is no great sin for large, complex organizations to receive complaints. The sin is not knowing that there is a problem, or not doing something about problems and learning lessons for the future. Similarly, if a person or department is doing well, the Board should know and add its congratulations or thanks.

Patient's Charter

We are in the early days of the 'Charter movement'. What is emerging is the power that Charters can have to improve quality. Purchasers are likely to place greater emphasis on the importance of complying with local and national standards. The Board needs to know what progress is being made and what problems Charters are creating.

Financial performance

Such factors as cash balances and income expenditure are dealt with elsewhere in this book. The financial performance of the organization is the Board's primary responsibility. Many factors contribute to the financial success of the organization. They include: activity, utilization, staffing, quality and risk. The Board will wish to be sure that it has enough information to know what is going on and what is likely to happen.

Index

00000735